Something Fishy

poems by

Vicki Iorio

Finishing Line Press
Georgetown, Kentucky

Something Fishy

Copyright © 2018 by Vicki Iorio
ISBN 978-1-63534-660-2 First Edition
All rights reserved under International and Pan-American Copyright Conventions.
No part of this book may be reproduced in any manner whatsoever without written permission from the publisher, except in the case of brief quotations embodied in critical articles and reviews.

ACKNOWLEDGMENTS

With thanks and gratitude to the editors of the following publications where some of these poems first appeared:

Clowns, Goldfish and Dummies, *Home Planet*
The Icthyologist's Mother, *Cactus Heart Press*
From One Girl to Another, *The Fem*
The Vocabulary of a Hurricane, first appeared in my chapbook, *Send Me a Letter*, dancinggirlpress
Next Time Around, *The Long Island Quarterly*
The Astronaut, *The Brownstone Poets Anthology*

Publisher: Leah Maines
Editor: Christen Kincaid
Cover Art: Josef Krips
Author Photo: Kaetie Weigland
Cover Design: Elizabeth Maines McCleavy

Printed in the USA on acid-free paper.
Order online: www.finishinglinepress.com
also available on amazon.com

Author inquiries and mail orders:
Finishing Line Press
P. O. Box 1626
Georgetown, Kentucky 40324
U. S. A.

Table of Contents

I Give My House Keys to My Ex 1

Clowns, Goldfish and Dummies 2

Pop-eye 4

A Keeper 5

Recipe for a Hurricane 6

The Vocabulary of a Hurricane 7

Irma's Eye 8

Next Time Around 9

My Father Marries Diana Nyad 10

Mermaid Season 11

Please Come Drinking with Me 12

The Ichthyologist's Mother 14

Stockholm Syndrome 15

Your Doctor's Bill is Ready for my View 16

He Dies 18

Neptune Society 19

Beach Marker 20

The Astronaut 21

From One Girl to Another 22

To Venus 24

Catch a Big One, Billy Bob 25

I dedicate this chapbook to Hurricane Sandy who forced me to swim with the fishes in my drowning basement. And to the poet Deborah Hauser, my doppelgänger, my shimmering mermaid who saves my poetic life every day.

I Give My House Keys to My Ex

After the tidal surge
I check the basement.

A colony of fish swims in and out
of volumes of George Bernard Shaw.

Minnows dart in the salt water swirls
of my Maytag drum.

No longer Downy Fresh, clothes locked in the spin
cycle smell of blood and iron.

Toenails plucked from my waterlogged feet
are painted beetles floating toward their destiny.

A big fish lurks in the cave of the stairwell;
as two huge pupils prey on me

and dinosaur fins whirlpool my furniture.
The old television tube is oranged with goldfish.

I tell my ex he can take back the house
I won in the divorce.

He wants the complete works of Shakespeare,
a gift from one of his girlfriends.

I leave the keys under the mat.
The cat and I take a Southwest flight to a dry climate.

Without benefit of electricity,
rising water marries him to the ecosystem of my drowned life.

Clowns, Goldfish and Dummies

I learned to pee with clowns.

Perpetual clown tears drip from primal blue eyes
drop off red noses, land on yellow clown shoes.
Emmett and Bozo blessed the walls of my bathroom.
Most nights, I chose wet sheets over these witnesses.

*

My uncle found a ventriloquist's dummy
while on patrol at the end of his war.

When he lived with us, he'd sit on the closed toilet seat,
dummy on his knee and practice throwing his voice
in the echo our bathroom made,
performing for an audience of clowns.

Ma made me sit with them so she could smoke in peace.
The dummy's wooden body bone- rattled when it told me its secrets.

*

I killed goldfish.
Science project went belly up.
Fish overfed in the morning
died in the afternoon.

Anemic blood starved vampire teacher
made me take their exploded little corpses home
in my lunch box that still smelled of tuna.
I flushed my failure down the toilet.
Judging clowns, unicycle Jesuses cried for my sins.

*

Coming home with our newborn, my husband gifts me
a wall to wall aquarium crowded with
sneering armies of clown fish.
My uncle's dummy, polished to a high shine,
sitting on a kitchen chair in front of the tanks
welcomes me home with a crooked bouquet.

Pop-eye

Coins iridescing in the summer sun or shiny
pebbles on the pier. Before the little girl really sees
them, she grabs her treasure. Upon discovery,
she flings from her hands fish eyes that attach
to the fibers of her cheap knit shorts.

Her father washes her hands in the same bloody
water that buckets the caught fish, flicks
off the eyes from his daughter's clothes,
calls her stupid.

Exophthalmia, a condition of betta fish. Her father
makes her scoop out the affected, feel
their coldness, watch angels panic
before they are isolated in a nurse tank.
Ichthyophobia: icthys, the ick factor.

Daddy, fish are icky.
He peppers her food with fish fins,
puts a dead fluke in her Christmas stocking.

A Keeper

Because I keep a mermaid in the basement
I wash her delicate sequined pink bra in the bathroom sink

gingerly scrub around her clam shells
with a soft toothbrush fresh out of its wrapper

Because I keep a mermaid in the basement
I have not done the work left me by a hurricane

She is a blue flame phosphorescence
illuminating the basement in ways electricity never could

Because I keep a mermaid in the basement
I tell my nosy neighbors I am still waiting for FEMA
when the ask me about the standing water and the flickering lights

Because I have named the mermaid in my basement Jayne Mansfield
I have to rethink my sexuality

Jayne flips me her dorsal fin
swims deep and reads drowned books
learning the language they teach her

I tell her I will buy a wet suit
and take her back to the midnight ocean

Recipe for a Hurricane

At the first rap get the vodka
it is not a gentle rap like the raven's
it is damnation
Look for the grenadine before the final flicker
it is there among the dusty bottles left by
disappointed exes
Chin up, gin up, floods of stoicism
when the water pools around your neck
Grab the Bacardi before it drowns
into the carpet bottom
The world is a blue liqueur
with stars of angry books
dive bombing into the drink
Remember the triple sec
find a lantern glass among the
floaters
Gulp it down in equal parts

The Vocabulary of a Hurricane

Charge deep into this windswept sandy hurricane
cross north to south to hurricane

A tantrum of trees fall without permission
a battery of flood cars, rip outs, tossed liquor bottles brandy this
    hurricane

No logic to the damage, some houses are perfect candled by television,
others are black eyes, a boat sits on a couch modus operandi of this
    hurricane

And here is *Pancho's Cantina*, cleaved. Tacos, plates, salad into the street
blame it on God or nature or just the pure grande of this hurricane

Vicky, an armored mermaid pumps out seawater and minnows
throws down the gauntlet to this violent no Gandhi of a hurricane

Irma's Eye

Irma, a douche of a hurricane.
She makes me evacuate an overflow of scare

that does not flush when the water table
rises with the tidal surge.

We take the cat and flee to the Volusia Fair Grounds.
Two Jews walk into a shelter with beach chairs and a cat.

We are there among the kindness
of Christians playing guitars

and singing how God will save us all.
Under sour breath, I whisper, if there were a god why would

this happen. My sister elbows me, reverts to Pig
Latin to shut me up. We take the Red Cross coffee and the sleeping bags

and hope that Irma is a pussy cat.
I want to go home to Long Island where I understand the language.

The old Key West hippie distracts me with stories of past hurricanes
with exotic names. His voice is a poem.

His gnarly feet manly in pink flip flops, the blond hairs
on his tanned arms are a different planet than his long gray beard.

He is the crusher of my wet monster,
uncurls the scoliosis of palm trees and soothes

this hell hath fury with the tenderness
of his Southern charm.

Next Time Around

Because no one needs a poet
in a hurricane
I am coming back as a plumber.

Everyone will want a piece of me
when I arrive at your destruction
in a spotless white panel truck

armed with a shining tool kit.
I will snake out your overflow,
auger your inner core, unclog

your fears. As I crouch in ass crack stance
replacing your ballcock, my perfect schism
(beribboned in a metallic thong)

will make you hopeful. After I dredge
the basement, remove fish, I will
install red hot nipples on your gas line.

Unpeel when I am done, take a hot shower,
consider my invoice my magnum opus—
next time around.

My Father Marries Diana Nyad

My father never wanted to leave the water
My mother a jellyfish
Never let my father back in-

without a shark cage
without swim fins
without a life jacket

Suicide my mother's safety net

My father and Diana Nyad swim
One hundred miles
Easy for dolphins

Diana wears a seaweed veil
My father sings her Spanish songs
As they push off from Cuba
And swim to far away

Mermaid Season

Mermaid Season is a deadly season
great whites are devoured by full lips
Long Island old salt poet   haunted

by one particular mermaid   followed her
from Brooklyn to the North Sea
called her Mata Hari   knew she was no good

pea-coated with a bottle he marlin brandoed
the waterfronts for her   grabbed her tail
a shimmer of diamonds and emeralds

an Aladdin's cave of riches
she took him for a ride   whiplash in a whirlpool
now crazy he only writes about Mermaid Season

that tuna smell   tail specificity
his wife has DNAed the slime in his pockets
the results have come back   origin unknown

the cat knows the origin   hears the high pitched mewl
stays away from canned fish
the many weeks of Mermaid Season

Please Come Drinking With Me
For D.H.

Let's meet at the Southeast corner of High Street
    I will watch your witchy shoes
    step ladylike out of the subway

Let's go to Melville's Liquors
    howl like banshees through the aisles
    make the watchful proprietor nervous

Let's study the names of wines from exotic places
    buy a silvery white from South Africa

Let's go down to Brooklyn Bridge
    unpeel pantyhose-the October sun is warm
    play in the flood-tide

Let's christen this day with an oaky chardonnay
    bottled in a waxed carton
    as innocent as mother's milk

Let's raise our skirts
    moon the ferry-boats
    listen for the camera clicks of tourists

Let's get blurry and reimagine the Twin Towers
    toast The Watchtower's conversion to condos
    the bridge traffic   the couples locking in their love
    on steel cables

Let's spy Walt ruin his boots walking on the river bank
    scratch at his beard while birthing poems
    search for a sailor's bar

    Let's say a wine prayer for the Sandhogs
        Reach into my coat pocket
        I have the discreet-as-a-tampon flask you gave me

Let's warm up with a blood red cabernet- the sun is going down
        let's trade our petticoats for mermaid fins
        leave our pumps as a footnote on bruised rocks
        push off the granite and dive into the drink

The Ichthyologist's Mother

Sylvia discovers psychotropics   exchanges winter for a tropical isthmus
Auntie   a joyful black moon   warms all of Sylvia in her big hands

Auntie puts color into this white girl   weaves a floppy purple orchid
through Sylvia's stringy blond hair

Auntie watches over Sylvia   dresses her in sarongs   burns the twin sets
in the oven   buries Sylvia's cold pearls   spells their voodoo

Sylvia's children make sand castles   the boy sculpts a fish   details fins
with a plastic spoon   Squinting in the sun he searches the turquoise
for a porpoise or a whale   on whose back   he can ride away

His sister crushes his creation with a rusty shovel   he does not forgive
this betrayal

Sylvia finds her strength   serves her husband divorce papers
the last thing   she will ever serve him
he cries behind stiff British doors   he never writes another good line

Sylvia crafts another collection   it is a colossal success   Her children
grow up   She leaves the island to visit her son in Alaska
Auntie tends the cats

Sylvia admires the fish tanks   Her son studies so many varieties   so
much science   The forced heat in this Fairbanks lab
dries out Sylvia's golden skin

When the disease comes the fish die   her son dies
from the rope of his biology

Stockholm Syndrome

Blue crab trapped by fi(ni)shing line
big claw surrendered to the wire
desiccated carapace one with his captor

When you were just days old
Anthony brought me blue crabs to cook
I forced those Atlantic swimmers

into the covered stockpot with one hand
while the other guided your mouth
to my breast to stave off hunger

Your Doctor's Bill Is Ready for my View

He's put you in a clinic
the one in Massachusetts
the one for anorexia

result of your drinking
or heroin
or was it an overdose of Vitamin B
it's all so confusing

He called at 2am
I can usually tell when he had one too many
the slurred words   his drunk-singing Sinatra used to
make me wet

He asked me for money
said it's all in the family, really
Really?

If he wasn't drunk it's worrisome
told me when his ship comes in
he's going to learn to sail and just drift

away   Did he ever take you under Goose Neck Bridge
in his Boston Whaler   drink tequila
wait for the tug   The wake

made me vomit into the same pail
with the shitting and dying fluke
He called it a Day of Death

You helped him find Jesus
poor Jesus
is mazel tov in order?

He's a vegetarian now
another one of your conversions
I still enjoy meat   assured that I am
a lobster on the cosmic plate

Tuesday night he was trawling off the dock
Four Roses and a pea coat
now His Holiness throws back his catch

He dies

and they want to know
which wife was I

the bow legged crone
wrapped in black tights and clogs

the bitter olive
with a sharp stone

the barbed wire heart
with picket fence bones

the purple jellyfish
stunning tentacled bride

the murderous crow
feasting on dead eyes

the aggressive algae
blooming a red tide

which wife was I

Neptune Society

Flat on the floor of your boat
arms crossed on my chest I am
a mythic queen on her death journey.
You are my oarsman. I cannot sight land for you.

The blue ceiling above blackened
by pelicans hunting for food
and your hairy toes below, yellowed by fungus,
are my anchors.

In this dying, my heart is a caught bass—
breaking free from the hook.
You are my captain. You push
my body overboard.

Cocooned in fish kisses, my flesh is recycled.
Parts of me, stuck to a rock—a drowned stump,
wash up on shore. You chart
the shock of my bones.

Beach Marker 414

My sister still bikini rocks it, I use tattoos as a distraction.
We drink painkillers at Joe's Bar and Grill. Island lesbians are
fashion forward in sports
bras and boxers. Someone who looks like my spin instructor
is playing beach volleyball. Her diamond studs, a singular sun. I
want to
lick the salt around her ear lobes.

A purple flag designates marine life. All life is
dangerous. A hazardous waste. Driving to New Hampshire, in my
winter,
I pass a town on I91 called Hazardville. I should just stop driving
and plant my tentacles there.

Physalia, a man-of-war, blue bottle floating terror.
Asexual killers of fry are toxic. Cancer made my sister a widow.
My rack and pinion has lost its swivel. I no longer drive on the
beach.
Wear flip flops on the purple days.

The Astronaut

In the Bealls Outlet parking lot I back up into his Saturn
        Hot day in Titusville smells like dead trout

Challenger circled by stars
        a patch on his flight jacket   USA
engraved on his space helmet bakes in the backseat sun
        a broiling aorta

This traveler makes my heart a truant
        to my obligations   He tells me not to

fret   the car a government rental   We eat raw tuna
        at a sushi bar   Later under a full moon he traces Ursa

Minor on my majors   mixes Tang with Vodka   orbits my O
        rings   makes my g-forces soar

Proves astrophysics is an art

From One Girl to Another

And from that day on everything seems different. At first you feel new and strange.....the way a butterfly must feel when it suddenly discovers it has wings

Nine year old summer. I fall out of a tree. After disposal of buds and twigs, the cleansing of wounds, a deeper blood remains.

Girls have some crazy names for it: my friend, the monthlies, Aunt Flo, grandma coming to visit, falling off the roof, getting the pie

My mother tosses me a box of Kotex. Tells me to stay in my room.

Have an excuse when the boys ask you to go swimming...you can don your play suit and get a tan while the others swim. Don't tease the boys they might throw you into the briny

I am a fish but mom won't let me near the water. When my best friend Robert, my pool pal, his lunch wrapped in a beach towel, comes to get me, Ma slams the door in Robert's face.

And you need never feel the least embarrassed to ask for a Kotex in a store—even if it's a tall, young red-haired lad on the other side of the counter. He'll give you a box of Kotex without batting an eye.

Yeah right

Tampons and the 'internal' method. Frankly most authorities say most young girls shouldn't use tampons without first consulting their doctors........a brush with the hymen

Ma pounds on the locked bathroom door. "Are you using a Tampax?" Threatens to call my father or the fire department.

Keep your hair clean and tidy. Wear fresh clothes......sprinkle Quest powder on the pad to stop the odor, this will give you poise and make you more attractive

By age 13, I go with the flow, don polka dot frocks, go under the boardwalk with boys.

If you depend on your memory you're sure to get mixed up..... If you stop for an overlong time then check with your mother and go to the doctor for a good frank chat. He can probably fix you up in time

Or call you a stupid girl.

Text, From One Girl to Another, puberty and menstruation booklet from Kotex Sanitary Napkins, 1940

To Venus

Latin root, venerari-to try to please.
Vener-my last name.
Girls, try to please.
Hilary Clinton apologized when she lost the election.
I said I'm sorry when I made boys come outside of me.
Origin of sorry is sore.
Sex is more pain than full.
Venus took a bath and became a virgin again and again.
Why would she do that?
Is this a case of goddess pleasing?
Oh please.
Some girls pretend they are mermaids to protect
their maidenhood. Maidenhood sounds like a hat worn at a royal wedding.
Put a feather on it or wear a burka for further protection.
The mermaids I know fuck through a shimmering slit.
Virginity is no biggie under the sea. Tides pop that cork.
Venus came out of the sea on a clamshell.
Baked clams are an aphrodisiac.
Venusaur is a poisonous Pokémon, with bumpy blue skin.

Catch a Big One, Billy Bob

Sunday mornings, hung over, my boyfriend and I watch fishing shows on television.
It is the 1970's B.C. (before cable). It is either religion or the fish.

Bookended on the sectional, we watch Billy Bob slice through the fresh waters of Georgia,
cast his rod and bring up largemouth bass or other prehistoric things.

At the beginning of each show the boat captain says, *Catch a big one, Billy Bob.*
Sea sick from tequila, I have a bag of ice cubes on my belly, wet towels turban

my head. Saturday nights we clink Jose Cuervo bottles, shout, Catch a big one, Billy Bob,
and suck down the worm. Daylight slashes through broken Venetians, glares the television.

My boyfriend asks me for a sardine sandwich. I crawl into the kitchen,
order my vomit to stay down like the bad dog it is. By noon, on a somewhat even keel,

I am strong enough to go to bed. My boyfriend wraps me in a blanket the color of
Georgia fresh water. With sardine breath, he lullabies me with a whisper of

Catch a big one, Billy Bob.

Vicki Iorio is the author of the poetry collection, *Poems from the Dirty Couch*, Local Gems Press, 2013 and the chapbook, Send me a Letter, dancinggirlpress. You can read Iorio's work in *Hell strung and Crooked, I Let Go of the Stars, (Great Weather for Media), The Brownstone Poets Anthology, The San Pedro Review, The Mom Egg, Crack the Spine, The Painted Bride Quarterly, The Fem Lit Magazine, Redheaded Stepchild Magazine, The Paper Street Journal, Poetry Bay, Home Planet News, Concise, Cactus Heart, Rattle on line, South Florida Poetry Journal, 521 Magazine, RatsAss Review, New York Times, blog site, 823 on High, Poetry Super Highway, Eratio Poetry Journal, In Between Hangovers, Conch.es, Anti Heroin Chic, Misfit, Califragile Poetry, Poetry Pacific, Carcinogenic Poetry., (b) OINK zine* and *puchdrunkpress.*

www.ingramcontent.com/pod-product-compliance
Lightning Source LLC
LaVergne TN
LVHW041517070426
835507LV00012B/1633